Newsmakers™

Pervez Musharraf

President of Pakistan

Daniel E. Harmon

ROSEN
PUBLISHING®

New York

Published in 2008 by The Rosen Publishing Group, Inc.
29 East 21st Street, New York, NY 10010

Library of Congress Cataloging-in-Publication Data

Harmon, Daniel E.
Pervez Musharraf: president of Pakistan / Daniel E. Harmon.—1st ed.
    p. cm.—(Newsmakers)
Includes bibliographical references and index.
ISBN-13: 978-1-4042-1905-2
ISBN-10: 1-4042-1905-6
1. Musharraf, Pervez—Juvenile literature. 2. Pakistan—Politics and
government—1988—Juvenile literature. 3. Presidents—Pakistan—
Biography—Juvenile literature.
I. Title.
DS389.22.M87H37 2007
954.9105'3092—dc22
[B]
                                                  2006039717

On the cover: President Pervez Musharraf of Pakistan. Background:
In 2006, special guards from Pakistan's armed forces commemorate
Defense Day in Rawalpindi.

CONTENTS

INTRODUCTION

Passengers aboard Pakistan International Airlines Flight 805—many of them school children—were increasingly nervous. Some verged on panic. Even the flight crew looked pale and worried. They had settled for a routine landing when the aircraft had abruptly nosed upward. Now it was making erratic course changes.

It was early in the evening of October 12, 1999. The airliner was scheduled to land at Karachi, a city on Pakistan's coast. Aboard was General Pervez Musharraf, chief of the Pakistan

Pakistani soldiers loyal to General Musharraf take control of the state television building in Islamabad during the bloodless coup of October 12, 1999.

army and chairman of the Joint Chiefs of Staff Committee. He was returning to his country aboard the commercial jet from Sri Lanka, an island nation in the Indian Ocean. On board the flight were almost 200 other passengers.

At 6:45 PM, Musharraf was quietly summoned to the cockpit. The pilot informed him that air traffic control in Karachi had radioed that the plane could not land there. This was not all: it was forbidden to land anywhere in Pakistan. The pilot had been ordered to leave Pakistani airspace immediately. The Karachi airport tower official would offer no explanation and would not suggest alternative airports.

"I could not believe what I was hearing," Musharraf recalls in his 2006 book, *In the Line of Fire.* "It seemed preposterous." The plane had enough fuel to remain in the air only an hour longer. This refusal to land as scheduled, Musharraf asserts, "was endangering a lot of innocent lives."

For the next forty-five minutes, tension mounted in the cockpit. The flight crew calculated the possibilities of reaching the nearest foreign airports on the limited fuel supply while Musharraf insisted on landing at Karachi. At one point, Karachi air traffic control told the pilot he could land at Nawabshah, a small Pakistani city 100 miles (160 kilometers) to the north. But soon after he diverted the airliner toward Nawabshah, the pilot was ordered to return to Karachi.

At about this time, an army officer in Karachi contacted Musharraf directly by radio. He informed his commander that the government two hours earlier had announced Musharraf's "retirement." Prime Minister Nawaz Sharif was trying to prevent him from returning to the country.

Musharraf's greatest anger was not that Sharif had terminated him while he was away, but that the pilot had been ordered to fly to an airport outside Pakistan. Low on fuel, the airplane might make it to Oman, on the opposite side of the Arabian Sea. Otherwise, it had to seek permission to land in neighboring India, Pakistan's bitter enemy. Musharraf considered this to be an act of hijacking and treason on the part of Sharif.

"It was a first in history," Musharraf states in his memoir, "an aircraft hijacked in the air by someone on the ground, and not just someone but a prime minister sworn to protect the lives of his country's citizens."

Although Musharraf was stunned by this abrupt crisis in the sky, he could not have been totally surprised by the unfolding events. He and Sharif had been on dangerously tense terms for months. Musharraf and other army officers had

begun discussing a possible coup d'état after
Sharif had interfered with army operations in the
province of Jammu and Kashmir earlier that year.
They claimed Sharif had forced them to abandon
a position in which Pakistan, after many years of
fighting, finally held a military advantage over India.

Even while the plane was in the air, officers and
soldiers loyal to Musharraf secured control of the
Karachi airport. This allowed the plane to land
there—with only a few minutes of fuel remaining.
Other military units, meanwhile, were rushing to
the aid of their deposed chief. They were in the
process of taking over the government from
Sharif and giving control to Musharraf.

Sharif later would be tried and exiled for
hijacking and other charges. Pakistan, a nation at
the stormy center of some of the world's most
challenging and dangerous problems, was under-
going a swift, dramatic change in leadership at
the dawn of the twenty-first century. Musharraf
has pointed out, in his memoir, that "the story of
my life coincides almost from the beginning with
the story of my country."

CHAPTER ONE

BIRTH OF A LEADER, BIRTH OF A NATION

Pervez Musharraf was born on August 11, 1943, in Delhi, India. He had an older brother, Javed; a younger brother, Naved, would come later. At the time of Pervez's birth, his family lived in the large home that had belonged for many years to his father's family. They called it Nehar Wali Haveli, which means "House Next to the Canal."

Several of his ancestors were government officials. A great-grandfather was a tax collector, and a grandfather was a judge. His father, Syed Musharrafuddin, was an accountant who worked for the foreign office of the Indian government. In time, his father became accounting director. Pervez's mother, Zarin, unlike most Muslim women, graduated from college and even earned a master's degree. She became a school teacher.

Pervez's father was a devout Muslim whose ancestors claimed to be descended directly from the prophet Muhammad. Pervez would continue to follow Islamic teachings throughout his life, but not as stringently as some of his forebears.

During these first years of his life, the people of India were clamoring for independence. Similarly, people in many areas of the world were rising up to end the era of colonialism. For centuries past, Great Britain, France, Germany, and other European powers had occupied and controlled vast distant lands to maintain trade privileges and military advantages. Throughout the early and mid-1900s, they were forced to give up control over their foreign colonies, one by one.

In India, the struggle for independence was especially complicated and savage. Muslims in the north of India wanted more than independence from foreign rule: they wanted an independent Muslim nation set apart from the rest of India, where the population is mainly Hindu. They would get their nation—Pakistan—but at a very high cost in human lives and suffering.

CLASH OF RELIGIONS

To better understand the strife that has ravaged Pakistan and India since the time of Pervez Musharraf's birth, you need to know something of the region's history. Religion has been a driving force there since ancient times. The Indian peninsula, or subcontinent, has been populated mainly by followers of the Hindu religion for more than 2,000 years. In the northern part of the peninsula, however, Muslims have become dominant during the past few centuries. Their religion, Islam, originated in Arabia during the sixth century and spread across the Arab world. Actually, most of the Indian subcontinent was ruled by the Mughal Empire, which was rooted in Islam, for more than 300 years, until 1857.

By that year, the East India Company, a great English trading organization backed by the British government, had established a degree of control over what is now India and Pakistan. British India, as it was known, was said to be the "jewel in the crown" of the worldwide British Empire.

The movement for independence from Great Britain, led primarily by Mohandas Gandhi, came to a head after World War II (1939–1945). The land was torn hopelessly by religious differences. Muslims had become the majority in the northern regions but were the minority in India as a whole. The Hindu leadership in India insisted their new government would be secular, showing no favoritism toward any religion. Nevertheless, most Muslims did not want to live under a government controlled by Hindus. Led by Muhammad Ali Jinnah, they demanded a separate Islamic nation.

When it was created in 1947, Pakistan was a nation literally divided. To the northwest of India was West Pakistan—the Pakistan of today. It has a shoreline of several hundred miles on a sector of the Indian Ocean known

Muslim worshipers assemble at a mosque in Delhi, India, in 1946, near the end of British rule. The following year, Pakistan and India became separate, independent nations.

as the Arabian Sea. From the coast, it extends in a ragged, narrow band northeastward about 1,000 miles (1,609 kilometers) to the China border. Afghanistan is its neighbor on the northwest, Iran on the far west.

About a thousand miles to the east was East Pakistan. East Pakistan was much smaller, about a seventh the size of West Pakistan, but its population was approximately the same. Pakistan was considered a central homeland for Muslims in southern Asia.

Obtaining a separate Pakistan was not such a difficult matter. The dilemma was which areas of northern India would be part of Islamic Pakistan and which would be part of Hindu India. The boundary, fashioned primarily by the British, was badly drawn. It placed many Muslim villages in India, many Hindu and Sikh villages in Pakistan.

The greatest conflict between the neighboring countries, which continues today, concerns the border region of Jammu and Kashmir. At the time of independence, the leader of Jammu and Kashmir, Maharaja Hari Singh, wanted Britain to

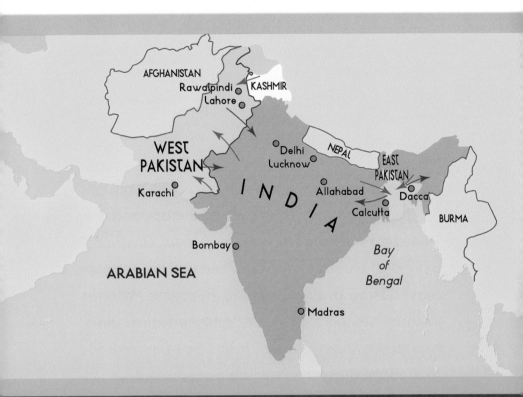

When Pakistan and India became independent in 1947, many Muslims living in northern India migrated across the border into the new nation of Pakistan; Hindus in Pakistan moved down into India.

grant his state its own nationality. The British government refused, requiring that all the border states become part of either India or Pakistan.

British rule ended at midnight, August 14, 1947. For Syed Musharrafuddin and his wife and their three sons, the height of the crisis came that same month, when Pervez was four years old. They, along with thousands of other Muslims living in the newly independent India, fled across the border into the newly independent Pakistan. At the same time, thousands of Hindus and Sikhs were fleeing Pakistan into India. Over a period of weeks, more than ten million people moved from one country to the other. Militants on both sides attacked the refugee trains and massacred those aboard. It has been estimated that approximately a million people died; countless more were robbed, raped, and injured. The young family feared for their lives as they boarded a train in Delhi, bound for Karachi on the Pakistan coast, where relatives and friends hopefully would be waiting.

Muslims at a refugee camp in northern India await transportation to Pakistan at the time of independence and the division of the two countries in September 1947.

An Early Lesson in Forgiveness

When Pervez was about five years old, his family lived in a small, crowded apartment in Karachi. One night while his father was away, Pervez spied a strange man hiding behind their sofa. He tiptoed outside to fetch his mother. At the sound of her screams, neighbors hurried to their aid and captured the man, who was trying to steal a bundle of clothes. Some went for the police while others took justice into their own hands and beat him severely.

Their anger turned to pity, however, when the thief shouted that he was only trying to get something to wear and that he was starving. Pervez's mother was so shocked by his plight that when the police arrived, she told them the man had stolen nothing, so they let him go. She then prepared a hot meal for him!

Pervez Musharraf remembers that during those tough, uncertain first years of the new republic, refugees like his family were thrown together and relied on one another to make the best of life. They shared what they had, he recounts in *In the Line of Fire*, and there was a "sense of accommodation" among them.

Thankfully, their train made the journey unmolested. Although they had few possessions with them, they eagerly set about to build a new life in a new nation. Domestic life for them was hard, while international hostility strained past the breaking point. Fighting broke out in Jammu and Kashmir in October 1947. It escalated into the First Indo-Pakistani War, which lasted more than a year. The United Nations arranged a cease-fire and established a dividing "line of control" through the area. Approximately two-thirds of Jammu and Kashmir came under Indian control, a third under Pakistani control.

TIGHT QUARTERS

Life in Karachi for the family of Syed Musharrafuddin after "Partition," as Pakistanis and Indians refer to independence, was very different from the life they'd left in Delhi. They occupied two rooms in a barracks-like building. Their quarters included a kitchen area and a primitive toilet. It soon became extremely crowded because some of their relatives arriving

Muhammad Ali Jinnah, leader of the future Pakistan *(right)*, and Jawaharlal Nehru *(third from left)*, leader of the future India, address reporters at independence negotiations in 1946.

from India were placed with them in their small apartment. As many as eighteen individuals at a time lived in their little space. Other families were packed into nine similar units of the barracks.

Remarkably, Musharraf remembers, they rarely complained. Despite their hardships, they felt they had attained freedom and a new life. The most dangerous threats and tensions, they sensed, were behind them.

Pervez's parents were intent on providing their sons with the best education possible. They enrolled Javed and Pervez, the two oldest, in a school operated by Roman Catholic missionaries. The boys walked about a mile (a kilometer and a half) each way.

Their father was given a position in the Pakistan foreign office. Their mother became an inspector with the customs service. They did not make much money, but Pervez remembers those years as a happy time. They looked to the future and believed they were taking part in establishing a nation.

CHAPTER TWO

SCHOOL DAYS

In 1949, Pervez's father was assigned to the Pakistan embassy in Ankara, Turkey. He was placed in charge of the embassy's accounts department, and his mother became a typist on the embassy staff.

The family remained in Turkey seven years. They lived in houses that were not very big but far more comfortable than their crowded apartment in Karachi. They had relatives in Turkey, and they found the Turkish people quite friendly, so they quickly were made to feel at home.

The brothers at first attended a Turkish school, where they learned to speak the Turkish language fluently. Then their parents placed them in a private school. Among other subjects, Pervez learned English and excelled in math and geography. His interest in geography—the study of maps, oceans, rivers, mountains, deserts, and other types of terrain—gave him

A section of historic Ankara, Turkey, is seen here as it appeared In the late 1940s when Pervez Musharraf lived there as a child.

an early advantage in his future career as an army commander.

For recreation, he enjoyed gymnastics, badminton, volleyball, and other sports. He was a mischievous child—sneaking into the embassy orchard for fruit, playing marbles despite his mother's forbidding it—but he liked attending school.

He was not a particularly avid reader. Only much later, when he was a cadet at the Pakistan Military Academy (PMA), did he take a serious interest in books. He preferred to be outside, playing with friends. The neighborhood boys organized "gangs," each with its own flag, and waged mock battles. Pervez was good at arranging ambushes and plotting skirmishes. He was a natural leader.

A Tough Upbringing

Pervez Musharraf has described the section of Karachi in which they lived as a tough place. He joined a street gang and became, in his words, "one of the tough boys."

A bully in the neighborhood treated the other boys cruelly. One day when the boy tried to get kite string from Pervez's older brother, Javed, Pervez attacked the boy and beat him severely.

"The lesson I learned," Pervez recalls, "was that if you call a bully's bluff, he crumbles. The secret is to stand your ground for a few seconds, and your initial fright vanishes."

Mustafa Kemal Atatürk reviews some of his Turkish troops in 1922. Atatürk helped establish modern Turkey; he is one of Musharraf's role models.

During his childhood in Turkey, Pervez became deeply interested in the life of Mustafa Kemal Atatürk, who led Turkey to independence during the 1920s. Atatürk is considered the "father" of modern Turkey. Pervez was impressed by his example of leadership. Even today, he speaks respectfully of Atatürk. Turkey was a new republic under Atatürk, just as Pakistan was a new republic when the Musharrafuddin family moved there.

Pervez became intrigued by the image of military officers at the embassy. He admired their neat, formal uniforms. One of the officers befriended Javed and Pervez. He took them on long hikes and coached them in developing sports skills. Pervez decided at an early age that he wanted to become an army officer. His mother encouraged his ambition; perhaps she thought it would harness his mischievous, over-active nature and put it to a worthwhile use.

Although his parents demanded respect for elders and often were angered by Pervez's boyish pranks, they themselves were not averse to having fun. They loved music and were excellent ballroom dancers. In 1953, in a ballroom dancing competition held to celebrate the crowning of Queen Elizabeth II of Britain, they won first prize.

While Pervez and his family were living in Turkey, Pakistan was experiencing crises and changes. Prime Minister Liaquat Ali Khan was assassinated in 1951. Overall, the government was not regarded highly by the people. Pakistanis believed many of their leaders were corrupt and ineffective. They placed more confidence in the military, which had been keeping the peace in local conflicts as well as protecting the national borders. Soon the army would exert control over matters of politics as well as defense.

The Musharraf family made many friends in Turkey and enjoyed life there. Pervez was very sad when, in 1956, his father was transferred back to the foreign office in Karachi.

RETURN TO PAKISTAN

Pervez was amazed at how large Karachi had grown. The family found a home in a new neighborhood and settled down once more. His mother, Zarin, got a job as a secretary at a factory. Pervez and his older brother, Javed, returned to the same Catholic missionary school they had attended when they were small.

A difficulty in Pervez's studies was the fact that he had a poor grasp of the widely used Urdu language. While he had learned Turkish well and could speak English, he had to be tutored in Urdu. He enjoyed school, but he continued to be a prankster and often got in trouble with his teachers. Javed was a model

The early years of independence were turbulent times in Pakistan. Liaquat Ali Khan, the new country's first prime minister, was assassinated by a Muslim fanatic in 1951.

student who received top grades. Pervez was an average student—and his grades took a nosedive in class ten (tenth grade), when he fell in love and lost all interest in everything else. The romance ended when his family moved to a different part of the city.

The school system in Pakistan is different from that in the United States. The eleventh and twelfth classes (grades) in Pakistan are college classes. In 1959, Pervez's parents sent him to the Forman Christian College, an American missionary institution in Lahore, to complete his basic education. He already knew he wanted to join the army, and he was required to finish the college classes first.

COLLEGE POLITICS AND PRANKS

It was the first time Pervez had lived away from his family. Naturally, he was terribly homesick. He overcame it in part by throwing himself into athletics. He became the college's best gymnast and one of its fastest cross-country runners.

He got his first taste of politics at Forman Christian College. In his first year he ran for a student representative position—and won. But he did not enjoy the required speech-making.

And he continued his life as a prankster. One of his frequent tricks was to climb down a mango tree and sneak outside the college gates at night, which was forbidden. He and other daring students would go to a movie theater, spend the night in a mosque near the campus gate, and slip back inside after the gate was opened early the next morning.

On one occasion, he and friends placed three crude firecracker "time bombs" at several locations around the campus. One was in a trashcan, another in a mailbox. They exploded deafeningly, frightening everyone and bringing chaos to the campus.

The college warden questioned one of Pervez's friends and demanded to know who had led the "bomb plot." The boy faced expulsion if he did not tell. When Pervez learned of his plight, he insisted that his friend tell the truth and let Pervez accept the blame. Perhaps it was his confession that softened the warden's heart. After Pervez promised never to do it again, the warden let him go unpunished.

Before the end of his second year, Pervez was accepted at the Pakistan Military Academy. In 1961, he enrolled for the three-year training program. If he passed, he would emerge as an army officer.

CHAPTER THREE

A YOUNG SOLDIER

When Pakistan became independent in 1947, the veteran soldiers in its new army had served loyally under British command in India. They now served a new nation and its government. Although the country had no shortage of soldiers willing to defend it, it did have a shortage of qualified officers. In the British Indian army, most of the officers had been Hindus. Pakistan was forced to hire about 500 British officers to help lead its army of 150,000 soldiers, as well as its small air force and navy. In fact, the first two commanders in chief of Pakistan's armed forces were Englishmen. General Mohammad Ayub Khan, the first Pakistani to hold this high post, took over in 1951.

Establishing an effective military was important to Pakistan's new government leaders, who believed that the country was surrounded by threats. The national borders divided various groups of people who had shared ethnic and cultural ties for hundreds of years. Certain people from an ancient ethnic group found themselves in the new nation of Pakistan, while relatives lived in adjoining countries.

One result, which continues into the twenty-first century, is that many Pakistanis disrespect the official borders. Some Afghans, for example, refuse to accept the border between Pakistan and Afghanistan. Armed force was necessary for the government to protect national interests.

A forceful military also was needed to quell unrest inside the country. Tribes and ethnic groups vied—sometimes violently—for a share of control in the new government.

Pervez Musharraf began his training at the Pakistan Military Academy (PMA) in 1961, at age eighteen. The PMA is located in Kakul, a town in the frigid north of Pakistan not far from the Himalayas Mountains. The extreme cold made the training, which would have been rigorous in any climate, even more severe.

Musharraf admits to entering the academy as a poorly disciplined youth. He once got into serious trouble when he and other cadets,

Smartly attired Pakistani soldiers stand at attention during a 2004 ceremony. Impressed by uniformed professionals and drawn to excitement, Musharraf at a young age decided on a military career.

ordered to run 9 miles (14.5 km) as punishment for a uniform violation, took a shortcut in the route. Their instructors were watching them through binoculars from a distance. The cadets came close to being expelled, but in the end they were punished by being lowered in their class standings.

Nevertheless, Musharraf adapted well to taking orders and was determined to make a good soldier. Moreover, his attitude toward academics improved. He became one of the leading cadets. In sum, according to his memoir, he regards his training as a life-changing experience, like "being taken apart and put back together differently." He graduated from the academy as a second lieutenant—the lowest-ranking officer in the army—and was assigned to an artillery unit.

"SAVED" BY A WAR

The mischievous nature of Musharraf's childhood still was not cured. In 1965, a year into his army career, he went absent without leave for eight days. His regiment was stationed near Lahore, and he requested leave to visit his family in Karachi, a day's train ride away. When his commanding officer refused, he went home anyway. He was about to be court-martialed, but international circumstances intervened. Pakistani-backed guerrilla activities in Jammu and Kashmir that September prompted attacks by Indian forces. The result was the Second Indo-Pakistani War.

During the seventeen days of fighting, which ended in a stalemate, almost 4,000 Pakistani soldiers died. Musharraf's artillery regiment was involved in heavy fighting in different parts of Pakistan. One night an Indian artillery shell landed on a heavy gun under Musharraf's command, setting it ablaze. If it exploded, he knew, it could blow up their other guns, as well. While most of his men fled for cover, Musharraf and one soldier took off their shirts and disarmed the flaming gun.

Rather than being court-martialed, Musharraf was pardoned and earned a medal for gallantry. Not long afterward, he was promoted to captain. His superiors realized that although he was a maverick, he was daring and smart—a good field commander.

COMMANDO FIGHTER

The following year, Musharraf decided to alter his army career. He wanted to become a commando, so he joined the army's Special Services Group (SSG). This required special training of an extremely challenging nature. Besides being in top physical condition, commandos had to master survival skills and be able to live in dangerous terrain, cut off from the main army, indefinitely. They learned to eat wild plants and animals—including lizards and snakes. They had to run as far as 36 miles (58 km), carrying a weapon and a 30-pound (13.6-kilogram) pack. They parachuted from planes and forced their way through water-ways with dangerous currents.

Musharraf excelled in each phase of training and was rated near the top of his group. To him, mastering commando training was more a matter of mental control than physical power.

He served in the SSG seven years, rising to the rank of major. His men respected him because he led them into action rather than ordering them to go before him. He was one of the fittest men in his unit, and he would challenge his soldiers to contests of endurance. If they beat him—which they did occasionally—he would reward them with a cold drink.

Sehba Farid married the young officer Pervez Musharraf in 1968. She is shown here during an official state visit to Tokyo, Japan, in 2002.

Still, he continued to have problems with his own sense of discipline. He sometimes got into fights and disobeyed orders. This held him back from rapid advancement.

SETTLING DOWN

During his years as a commando, his family introduced him to a beautiful young woman named Sehba Farid. They were engaged for two years while he served far away in East Pakistan. Soon after their wedding in December 1968, he was stationed to a remote mountain town. The Musharrafs' daughter, Ayla, was born in February 1970 and their son, Bilal, in October

1971. Today they have four grandchildren. In adulthood, Ayla would become an architect; Bilal would move to the United States and start a technology company in Boston, Massachusetts.

Musharraf credits Sehba with gradually curing him of his rebellious nature and instilling in him a desire to improve himself. An excellent linguist, she also helped him perfect his English.

Early in their marriage, Musharraf was sent to war again. Friction had been building between peoples of the eastern and western divisions of the country. After East Pakistan was ravaged by a tidal wave in 1970 that killed 200,000 people, survivors blamed President Yahya Khan and officials in West Pakistan for slow relief. Although half the country's population lived in the east, they felt isolated and unequally represented in government.

The next year, a hotly disputed national election brought the discord to a crisis. Zulfikar Ali Bhutto in West Pakistan claimed the title of prime minister of the country, despite the fact that a rival in the east, Sheikh

An artillery soldier readies his weapon in East Pakistan during the 1971 conflict that resulted in a permanent separation between the two parts of the country.

Mujibur Rahman, received greater support. President Khan disbanded the Awami League, the East Pakistan political party that had won the majority of National Assembly seats. Rahman, the leader of the Awami League, was arrested.

East Pakistan revolted. Not surprisingly, India helped the East Pakistanis in their fight for independence.

Musharraf's assignment during the final months of 1971 was to prepare a new commando unit in West Pakistan for battle. By the time it was combat-ready, however, transportation had been severed between East and West Pakistan and it could not take part in the fighting. It was just as well for Musharraf: a million people died in the two-week war, and 90,000 Pakistani soldiers and civilians became prisoners in East Pakistan.

The result was East Pakistan's transformation into a new nation, Bangladesh. "What happened in East Pakistan," Musharraf laments in his book, "is the saddest episode in Pakistan's history." He blames the loss of East Pakistan on the nation's incompetent political and military leadership and, in part, on the United States' unwillingness to intervene on Pakistan's behalf.

PAKISTAN JUGGLES FOREIGN RELATIONS

Since independence, Pakistan had turned to the United States for surplus army equipment left over after World War II. The United States viewed Pakistan as an important ally in its anti-Communist global strategy. During the 1950s and 1960s, the United States sold Pakistan many weapons, including ships and planes. It also helped train Pakistan's military officers.

At the same time, America was nurturing important diplomatic ties with India, Pakistan's nemesis. When fighting had broken out between Indian and Chinese forces in 1962, the United States had sent military aid to India. The reason was that China, a Communist-ruled country, posed a threat to the United States in the Cold War.

Pakistan was also juggling international alliances. It has had to be mindful of its relations with all the world's superpowers. China's opposition to India, for example, caused Pakistan to view the eastern giant as a possible new ally.

Pakistan's foreign relations had become quite complicated. They were to grow more difficult as the twentieth century entered its final decades.

CHAPTER FOUR

PROMOTIONS AND CHALLENGES

By the time of the 1971 war, Pakistan—although a democracy—had been under military control for most of its existence. In 1958, President Iskander Mirza abolished the country's political system. He disbanded elected assemblies, outlawed political parties, and threw out the national constitution. Mirza placed General Muhammad Ayub Khan in charge of martial law. Within weeks, Khan overthrew Mirza's government and made himself president. Since then, most of Pakistan's leaders have been part of the military establishment or have been controlled by it. The people found that life was more stable under military leadership, so they offered no massive resistance.

One reason for the people's deep reliance on Pakistan's military is the constant fear of attack from India. Border fighting between Pakistani and Indian forces, especially in the disputed territory of Jammu and Kashmir, has

President Ali Bhutto of Pakistan and Prime Minister Indira Gandhi of India sign the Simla Agreement in 1972. Sadly, their negotiations failed to end border fighting.

been frequent, and tension has been constant. Over the years, an estimated 40,000 people have been killed in the ongoing "Kashmir insurgency," as it is called. (Interestingly, most casualties occur not from skirmishes or artillery fire but from the intolerable climate.)

In 1972, Indian and Pakistani leaders met in the mountain town of Simla and negotiated what is known as the Simla Agreement. Although both sides recognized the "line of control" and agreed to refrain from future fighting, the agreement did not achieve a permanent settlement. Skirmishing has broken out repeatedly along the dividing line.

Pakistan's part in the border, or "frontier," fighting has been controversial. While regular army forces repeatedly have engaged the Indian army, guerrilla or "paramilitary" fighters have also been involved. These soldiers are not part of the regular Pakistani army, but the army has provided them with material and support. In the closing years of the century, their role would become increasingly worrisome to international observers because of their extremist tactics and their independence from government control.

TOUGH SOLDIER, SERIOUS STUDENT

The Special Services Group of army commandos was sent to the northern areas of the country, in the Himalayas near the China border, after the 1971 civil war. Their primary mission was to monitor the movements of Indian forces in neighboring Jammu and Kashmir. Musharraf, by then a major, and his comrades traveled by jeep and mule and on foot through the difficult terrain and brutal cold. Although it was almost impossible to travel in winter, he kept his men

Soldiers guard an outpost in the frigid mountains near the border between Pakistan and India. Border fighting has taken thousands of lives on both sides since independence.

on maneuvers. He wanted to make a psychological impression on the Indian soldiers, who rarely ventured from their shelters during the coldest months.

In 1974, Musharraf was chosen to attend the distinguished Command and Staff College, located in Quetta. By now he was a serious student of military science, and he excelled. He received an important command as a brigade major based in Karachi. Among other missions, his brigade was sent into the rural Balochistan province to put down tribal revolts. Musharraf learned that he could resolve some of the conflicts not by force but by diplomacy, befriending tribal chiefs.

Other important assignments during this time did not entail conflict. A calamitous flood occurred in 1976 when heavy rains, combined with glacial melting, overflowed the Indus and other rivers. Musharraf assembled several hundred tribal warriors and jail inmates to repair a break in a canal.

A NATION UNDER MILITARY RULE

During the 1970s, Pakistan was slipping into political unrest. Zulfikar Ali Bhutto, appointed president and later prime minister after the Bangladesh war, won praise for his reform policies and foreign initiatives, such as his formal

Three Brushes with Death

Musharraf has come close to death many times. As a major with a commando force in 1972, he was serving in a mountain region, which presented natural dangers as well as combat threats. Two soldiers were killed in an avalanche. At the time, Musharraf and some of his comrades were scheduled to fly out of the area aboard a commercial plane. When the bodies of the dead men were recovered, Musharraf and another officer stayed behind to allow for the excess weight the bodies added to the flight. High in the Himalayas, the plane crashed into a glacier.

A similar incident occurred in 1988. President Zia ul-Haq initially chose Musharraf to become his military secretary but changed his mind and selected another officer. Soon afterward, the replacement officer accompanied the president's party aboard an airplane that crashed, killing them all.

On yet a third occasion, one of Musharraf's officers, a helicopter pilot, planned to give him a lift from army headquarters to a distant location where they both were bound. The pilot could not locate him at the scheduled lift-off time and took to the air without him. The helicopter went down, killing the pilot.

recognition of Bangladesh as a nation in 1974. But he repressed political opponents and was considered by some—including Musharraf—a despot. After a furiously disputed 1977 election, General Muhammad Zia ul-Haq, chief of the army, overthrew Bhutto's administration. Bhutto was tried and convicted for allegedly having a rival politician murdered, and he was hanged in 1979. Many Pakistanis considered Bhutto a martyr.

Zia imposed martial law and ran the country until 1988, when he was killed in a mysterious airplane crash. Musharraf during these years advanced into the upper ranks of Pakistan's military. In 1978, he was made lieutenant colonel. The next year he became an instructor at the Command and Staff College—a post in which he greatly improved his public speaking skills. He later was sent to take a special course at the National Defence College in Islamabad. In 1985, he was promoted to brigadier (the U.S. equivalent of brigadier general) and became an instructor at the National Defence College.

Although his career was progressing nicely, Musharraf was dismayed by many aspects of martial law. He particularly opposed one inhumane form of punishment: caning petty criminals, most of whom were poor. At the jail in Rawalpindi, he witnessed a caning for himself. The prisoner was stripped and tied to a frame with his arms and legs stretched painfully apart. The jailer took a running start and slammed the inmate's buttocks as hard as he could—so hard that after five blows the man was untied and collapsed in a faint, his flesh raw and bleeding.

Musharraf came away so disgusted he asked his commanding officer to have the punishment banned. His superior agreed. Musharraf has observed that martial law diverts the military from its main duties and makes it difficult for an effective return to civil government in the future.

In 1988, after Zia's death, Benazir Bhutto was elected prime minister of Pakistan. Her election was remarkable for several reasons: she won the office in a democratic election; she was only thirty-five years old; she was the daughter of Zulfikar Ali Bhutto, her tragic predecessor; and she was the first woman to head a modern Islamic nation. Ghulam Ishaq Khan was appointed president.

Musharraf was asked to consider becoming Bhutto's military secretary. He decided against the move, dissuaded by his commanding officer. It proved to be a wise refusal. The appointed president had the power to "fire" the prime minister. Two years later, President Khan removed Bhutto from office on claims of corruption. Had Musharraf joined her staff, his career probably would have been ruined. As it was, he continued to advance in the army.

He was sent to London, England, in 1990 to study at the Royal College of Defence Studies, a part of the Defence Academy of the United Kingdom. Upon his return in 1991, he was given the rank of major general. Soon afterward, he was named Pakistan's director general of military operations, working closely with the chief of the army.

During the 1990s, Benazir Bhutto *(right)* and Nawaz Sharif *(left)* opposed each other for leadership of Pakistan. Both served twice as prime minister.

RAPID CHANGES IN LEADERSHIP

Nawaz Sharif became the next prime minister. In 1993, Khan attempted to dismiss him, too, and to shut down the National Assembly. Pakistan's Supreme Court ruled that Khan's actions were unconstitutional. This placed the nation's leadership in crisis. Ultimately, both

Khan and Sharif resigned. In elections later that year, Bhutto was returned to the position of prime minister.

Again, her leadership was short-lived. The new president, Farooq Leghari, ousted her—once more on corruption charges—in 1996. The next year, Sharif was re-elected prime minister. Bhutto went into exile in the United Arab Emirates.

Musharraf's career seemed to have stalled. He had been promoted to lieutenant general in 1995. In 1997, however, he was bitterly disappointed when another officer was given the prestigious post of army chief of general staff, a post Musharraf believed should have been his. At that point, he imagined he had risen as far in the army as he would rise.

He was wrong. One evening in October 1998, Prime Minister Sharif abruptly summoned him to Islamabad, the capital city. General Jahangir Karamat, the army chief, had been forced to resign after delivering a speech that struck the prime minister as being critical. Sharif had chosen Musharraf as his new army chief.

CHAPTER FIVE

CHIEF OF THE ARMY

From the outset, Musharraf was leery of the prime minister who'd appointed him to the top army post. Musharraf, like many other army officers, resented the dismissal of their brother in arms over what they considered a minor mistake—if it was a mistake at all. Musharraf had come to regard Sharif as a repressive leader who ruthlessly established total control over the government. His abrupt dismissal of General Karamat, in Musharraf's opinion, violated Pakistan's constitution.

At first, the two men worked together reasonably well. Musharraf sensed, however, that Sharif's domineering style of rule at some point would force a change. He was appalled when Sharif ordered him to "court-martial," on a charge of treason, a newspaper editor who had been arrested after offending the prime minister. Musharraf refused, and the editor was freed.

Musharraf *(right)* greets Prime Minister Nawaz Sharif in the Himalayas Mountains in February 1999. By the end of the year, Sharif had been ousted and Musharraf had assumed leadership of Pakistan.

Sharif had weakened the authority of the appointed president so that a military coup would be the only way he could be removed from office. According to his memoir, Musharraf confided to his officers that they should work with the government but, if Sharif attempted another "humiliation" of the army by deposing its chief, they should be prepared to "react."

MORE TROUBLE IN JAMMU AND KASHMIR

The inevitable break between Sharif and Musharraf occurred less than a year later. It resulted from the increasingly complex fighting in the Jammu and Kashmir territory.

Prime Minister Sharif in early 1999 invited Indian prime minister Atal Bihari Vajpayee to meet in Lahore, capital of the Punjab province in Pakistan. Sharif hoped to improve relations between their countries. As a gesture of cooperation, they announced a transborder bus service between Lahore and Amritsar, a city not far away in northern India.

These overtures of peace were marred when it was discovered that mujahideen (which means "freedom fighters"), supported by Pakistani army units, stealthily had occupied the strategically important heights of the Kargil region. This is in the Himalayas Mountains in Jammu and Kashmir and includes Indian-controlled territory. By taking the Kargil high positions in winter, the Pakistani

PERVEZ MUSHARRAF: PRESIDENT OF PAKISTAN

forces had obtained a great advantage in the
territorial dispute. Musharraf, as chief of the
armed forces, believed his country had scored a
remarkable strategic victory, simply by his soldiers'
willingness to maneuver during the severe
mountain winter. He hoped this could be parlayed
into a border agreement favorable to Pakistan.

Skirmishes ensued, and fighting intensified
during the spring as India sent troops, artillery,
and aircraft into the area. Pakistan, in turn,
fortified its positions. The world watched
apprehensively, fearing the conflict could escalate
into another Indo-Pakistani war—this time,
perhaps, a nuclear war.

In July 1999, Bill Clinton, president of the
United States, pressured Sharif to withdraw
Pakistani forces from the Kargil mountains.
Sharif ordered the soldiers out and condemned
the wintertime maneuver as a military blunder
on the part of his army commanders, carried
out without his knowledge.

Musharraf, in his book, says he was angered not
merely by Sharif's order to pull back from Kargil
and give up the important military positions, but

by the way Sharif handled the situation. The prime minister reputedly decided to withdraw forces from the area despite the advice of Musharraf and others in the Pakistani government. Furthermore, Musharraf insists that Sharif had been aware of the Kargil operation from the beginning.

By some accounts, Musharraf himself favored withdrawing from Kargil because Pakistani forces were losing their advantage. Musharraf denies the claim.

Regardless, the riff between the two men was irreconcilable. Just as Musharraf was distrustful of Sharif, the prime minister had become distrustful of Musharraf.

THE COUP D'ÉTAT

There is disagreement as to who took the initiative to eliminate the other in the coming months. Some think that in September, Musharraf and his most trusted subordinates began plotting to overthrow Sharif in the event the prime minister fired Musharraf. Musharraf told Sharif plainly that he refused to be dismissed from service before his three-year term as army chief ended. Sharif reportedly was warned by his own staff and by the Clinton administration in Washington that Pakistan's military might revolt if Sharif tried to replace his army chief.

Musharraf, on the other hand, says that by September 1999, he believed he and Sharif had gotten over their differences. At the prime minister's invitation, he had accompanied Sharif on a pilgrimage to Mecca, the Islamic holy city. Sharif had given Musharraf additional authority, making him chairman of the military's Joint Chiefs of Staff Committee as well as chief of the army. Musharraf maintains that he and his junior officers never conspired to overthrow Sharif's administration. However, they admittedly were prepared to act in the event Sharif attempted to dismiss him from his post. "His was the coup. . . . The army's response was the countercoup," Musharraf writes in his memoir.

While Musharraf was in Sri Lanka in early October, Sharif decided to replace him with Lieutenant General Khwaja Ziauddin. The announcement was made on TV at 5:00 PM on October 12. Army commanders loyal to their

Soldiers take over Pakistan television facilities during the October 1999 coup. Prime Minister Sharif attempted to fire Musharraf from his army command, but the army toppled Sharif's government.

chief immediately ordered units to secure essential government offices. Musharraf learned of his "retirement" shortly before 7:00 PM, as the airliner returning him from Sri Lanka approached Karachi. His army's counter-coup already was well in progress. By 8:30 PM, in a swift, bloodless operation, officers had arrested

Sharif at his residence and effectively taken control of the government.

Sharif, in the following year, was tried for kidnapping, hijacking, and terrorism in connection with his denial of landing clearance for Musharraf's airplane. He also was accused of government corruption and giving away military secrets. Found guilty, he was sentenced to life in prison. Musharraf, currying international approval, permitted him to go into exile in Saudi Arabia—after paying the government more than $8 million for alleged corruption.

Musharraf's assessment is that the army coup was necessary to save the country. The economy was faltering, crime and terrorist acts among Muslim factions were increasing, and the people had lost confidence in Sharif's government.

REACTION TO THE TAKEOVER

Most Pakistanis reacted favorably to the news that Musharraf had assumed leadership. Sharif had not been a popular prime minister. The nation's economy truly was unstable, and many

Pakistanis did not trust Sharif. His administration was tainted with bribery and other forms of corruption.

Radical Muslims, however, did not view Musharraf's takeover favorably. They wanted a hard-line, Islamic-based government similar to the one established in Iran after that country's violent upheaval in 1979. They were aware that Musharraf is not a strict practitioner of Islam and is quite liberal, by Muslim standards. For example, he and his wife have pet dogs, considered unclean by Muslim fundamentalists, and Sehba does not wear the traditional covering, a hibab, in public.

Although Pakistan is an Islamic nation—created, in fact, as a haven for Muslims on the Indian subcontinent—Musharraf favors a comparatively tolerant government. In his first years of leadership, for example, he would try, unsuccessfully, to relax the Islamic blasphemy law. Under this law, people can be imprisoned and even put to death—without an investigation—if they are accused of insulting the Koran or the prophet Muhammad.

Women's Opportunities in Pakistan

What did Pervez Musharraf's rise to power mean for Pakistani citizens? For women, it may have signaled an expansion of rights and opportunities. Traditional Islamic teachings and customs have discriminated against women, depriving them of equal rights, educations, and career opportunities. Pakistan, by contrast, has had women occupy professional and government posts. It even has had a woman prime minister, Benazir Bhutto.

Musharraf, whose daughter, Ayla, is an architect, has spoken in favor of greater justice and freedom for women. After he established his government, he appointed a female education minister to his cabinet. Sixty of the 342 seats in the National Assembly are reserved for women. (Women can also run for other seats.) A "women's political school" was instituted to train women for public office; Musharraf says some 27,000 women had taken advantage of it by 2006.

In his book, *In the Line of Fire*, Musharraf laments the "tragic and shameful condition of women in our society." He holds that "political empowerment" is the solution because it "gives them a way to shape their own future."

Women listen to President Musharraf during a December 2006 speech at a convention in Islamabad. Musharraf has pushed for new laws giving Pakistani women greater protection and freedom.

Musharraf has made further attempts to improve women's status. In December 2006, he pressed for legislation that would ban forced marriages and secure inheritance rights for Pakistani women.

Fighting among Muslims, especially between Shia and Sunni extremists, has been a recurring tragedy throughout the Islamic world. It had occurred in Pakistan since independence, and it was sure to continue into the new century.

Indians, meanwhile, were fearful of Musharraf. Their government had been on open, if not exactly friendly, terms with Sharif. Indians considered Musharraf a dangerous enemy because of his military leadership in the Jammu and Kashmir conflict. They were particularly wary of his past ties with the mujahideen fundamentalist fighters. The Indian government alleged that he had worked with separatist fighters who had committed atrocities in Jammu and Kashmir. Musharraf acknowledged his moral support of the Muslim separatists but denied that his military assisted them.

Other nations cautiously watched to see what would happen with Musharraf in control. The United States, among other countries, initially condemned the army coup. Their great concern was that because Pakistan and India both possessed nuclear weapons, a devastating war could result from the change in leadership. The United States and Canada imposed economic sanctions against Pakistan, hoping to force Musharraf to quickly restore an elected government.

Relations between the United States and Pakistan would change dramatically less than two years later. The deadly terrorist attacks of September 11, 2001, would cast the two countries as close allies.

CHAPTER SIX

THE NEW HEAD OF STATE

To control possible panic over the sudden change in government, Musharraf declared a state of emergency and martial law. He suspended the work of the National Assembly, fearing its leaders might challenge his authority. He promised that public elections would be held and democracy restored, although he did not say when.

Musharraf quickly took steps to begin mending Pakistan's failing economy. He imposed new taxes on the wealthy classes and created the National Accountability Bureau (NAB) to investigate corrupt government activities.

Opponents, however, challenged his takeover in Pakistan's supreme court. Although it did not declare his action illegal, the court ordered him to schedule national elections by October 2002 and end military rule.

On June 20, 2001, Musharraf made himself president of Pakistan. He established district

Musharraf had himself sworn in as president of Pakistan in June 2001. Administering the oath of office was Irshad Hassan Khan *(right)*, chief justice of the country's supreme court.

governments and called for national elections to take place in October 2002. In April 2002, Musharraf set up a referendum, asking voters to support his leadership and extend his presidency until 2007. The referendum gave him the endorsement he wanted, although rivals charged that voting violations were committed.

Musharraf began making changes in Pakistan's constitution. He formed a National Security

Council, headed by himself. Perhaps most significantly, he gave himself the authority to disband the National Assembly and to appoint or replace the country's prime minister.

In October 2002, national elections were held for the office of prime minister, parliamentary (National Assembly) seats, and provincial government posts. Mir Zafarullah Khan Jamali was elected prime minister. Candidates who supported Musharraf won the greatest number of seats in the National Assembly.

RELATIONS WITH INDIA

The issue foremost in the minds of international observers was Musharraf's attitude toward India. Initially, he gave them cause for serious concern. Within weeks of taking over, Musharraf denounced the Lahore Declaration that had been reached earlier that year by Sharif and Indian prime minister Vajpayee. For the moment, practically no diplomatic relations existed between India and the new government of Pakistan. Yet, Musharraf's stance, while unyielding, seemed open. He declared that if India was hostile,

Pakistan would respond with hostility. On the other hand, if India desired peace, he was willing to negotiate. He also expressed a keen desire to resolve the dispute over Jammu and Kashmir. His opinion was that the people of the region should be allowed to vote whether to join Pakistan or India.

Within a year or two, Musharraf seemed to mellow toward India. He quickly dispatched relief to the Gujarat province of India after it was ravaged by an earthquake in January 2001. Later that year, he agreed to meet with Prime Minister Vajpayee in Agra, India, for what would be called the Agra Summit.

In July 2001, Musharraf and his wife went to India. He placed a wreath at the memorial in honor of Mohandas Gandhi in New Delhi. Gandhi, a Hindu, was the leader who had inspired the independence struggle with his "passive resistance" strategy. To the Indian people, this was a significant gesture. No previous Pakistani head of state had paid tribute at the Gandhi memorial.

During their trip to India in July 2001, Musharraf and his wife visited the famous Taj Mahal monument in Agra.

The Agra Summit achieved little. No formal agreement came from it, but observers were heartened that Musharraf and Vajpayee at least had established respectful relations.

A permanent solution to the Jammu and Kashmir dispute, however, appeared as remote as ever. During the 1990s, the border issue became more complicated. Militants in Jammu and

Kashmir had taken up arms against Indian security forces. Their activities have increased. Some of the insurgents want to create a new nation; others want Jammu and Kashmir to become part of Pakistan. Not surprisingly, the Indian government refuses to consider either course.

In addition to native militia, raids are conducted by mujahideen, Muslim "freedom fighters," from other regions. During the early 1980s, mujahideen soldiers were trained in Pakistan to fight against forces of the Soviet Union who at the time occupied Afghanistan, Pakistan's neighbor to the northwest. Musharraf himself reportedly helped train the mujahideen. The United States provided funding for them to resist the Soviets. In time, training camps in Pakistan turned out many Muslim fundamentalists who would become part of the Taliban, the Afghan regime committed to holy war, or jihad, against non-Muslim influences in the region.

After the Soviets withdrew from Afghanistan in 1989, the Pakistani government began diverting mujahideen fighters from Afghanistan to the Kashmir and Jammu frontier to engage the Indian army. But the mujahideen proved unpredictable, sometimes fighting among themselves and refusing to operate under the direct control of Pakistan's government. Some carried out terrorist acts against civilians.

RELATIONS WITH THE UNITED STATES

The airliner attacks against U.S. targets in September 2001 dramatically changed the course of modern history—not just in the United States but also in Pakistan and many other countries. They altered the nature of Musharraf's international diplomacy and redefined his role as a head of state.

Since independence in 1947, Pakistan's relations with the United States have been generally favorable but increasingly complex. Pakistan's army during the early years depended on the United States for military material and training assistance. America, however, did not want to alienate India, Pakistan's archenemy. Diplomats on all sides have had to negotiate delicate issues. In the 1965 war, the United States refused to side with Pakistan, insisting on remaining neutral. This angered Pakistani leaders, who began negotiating with China and other countries for assistance. Just as America's friendliness with India has caused friction in Pakistan, Pakistan's friendliness with China and certain Islamic nations has caused concern in America.

Eventually, the United States renewed its military support of Pakistan. In return, Pakistan let the United States maintain a vital military base in Pakistan.

After assuming leadership, Musharraf took steps to curb Pakistan's internal violence. He banned two extremist groups that had been operating against each other within Pakistan. At the same time, though, he supported the radical Islamic Taliban regime in Afghanistan.

This supportive relationship changed after September 11, 2001, when Muslim terrorists attacked the World Trade Center and Pentagon in the United States. By virtually all accounts, the mastermind behind the attacks was Osama bin Laden, leader of the Al Qaeda system of Muslim terrorist networks. Bin Laden was believed to be sheltered by the Taliban government in Afghanistan. He had created Al Qaeda to oppose the Soviets there during the 1980s. He then became a bitter antagonist of the United States during the Persian Gulf War in 1991, when American forces were based in Saudi Arabia. Bin Laden viewed both the Soviets and Americans as enemies of Islam. In his mind, Americans had invaded Islam's sacred space in Saudi Arabia and Iraq and were trying to exert control over the governments and peoples of Muslim countries.

When the United States began planning its war against terrorist operations after the 9/11 attacks, it pressed Musharraf for assistance. The United States needed to use Pakistani military bases for its overthrow of the Taliban regime in Afghanistan. It also wanted the Pakistanis to halt the passage of fighters, weapons, and other materials between Al Qaeda groups in Pakistan and Afghanistan, and to help locate and eliminate Al Qaeda operations.

Musharraf was thrust into the deadly crossfire that threatens his life and his government to this day. He had been on friendly terms with the Taliban leadership in Afghanistan. The Taliban had

Protestors in October 2001 demonstrate in support of Osama bin Laden and against Musharraf's alliance with the United States in the military campaign against terrorism.

sent fighters on behalf of Pakistan into the Jammu and Kashmir border dispute. Musharraf also knew his population included countless sympathizers of the Taliban and Al Qaeda, as well as other militant Islamic organizations opposed to U.S. policies. These people would be angered by a close alliance between Pakistan and the United States. The result for Pakistan could be a gravely unstable government and economy.

On the other hand, Musharraf himself seemed genuinely appalled by Al Qaeda's violent extremism. It was obvious to everyone that the Taliban supported and protected Al Qaeda leaders. Musharraf recognized that the United States was determined to take down the Taliban regime with or without his aid. If he did not cooperate, he could find himself in a worse position than if he did. Sanctions against his country would continue, depriving it of economic and military support. Ties between the United States and India likely would be strengthened.

A week after the terrorist attacks on American soil, Musharraf announced to his people that they must support the international campaign against terrorists. He assured them that the U.S.-led war on terror was not a war against Islam but was directed specifically against terrorist operations.

Thousands of Pakistanis publicly protested the decision. They burned effigies of Musharraf and President George W. Bush in the streets. Most Pakistanis apparently agreed with Musharraf, and the protests diminished. Some Pakistanis, however, strongly protest his close alliance with America even today. "September 11, 2001," he writes in his memoir, "multiplied Pakistan's challenges many times over, amplifying domestic issues, and reshaping our international relations."

By the end of the year, Afghanistan's Taliban government was driven from power. This now compounded Musharraf's internal problems, for countless Taliban soldiers made their way across the border into Pakistan.

Tension with India, meanwhile, worsened. Terrorist attacks against Indian targets in 2001 and 2002 raised the specter of a nuclear war. Pakistan blamed the violence on independent militants based in Jammu and Kashmir. India claimed they were aided by Pakistan's military.

Both sides sent more soldiers into the region. World powers, including the United States, pressured the two governments to diffuse the crisis. In November 2003, Pakistan and India agreed to a cease-fire along the Kashmir dividing line, where opposing artillery units had fired on each other periodically since 1989. On one of Pakistan's troubled borders, at least, a respite had been achieved.

CHAPTER SEVEN

A DANGEROUS ROLE ON THE WORLD STAGE

"Dabaa! Dabaa!" Pervez Musharraf's desperate cry in Urdu—"Drive! Drive!"—spurred his driver to stomp the accelerator of the presidential Mercedes. The armor-plated car had been blasted into the air by a stupendous explosion but had landed intact. A van containing explosives had been driven by suicide bombers into Musharraf's motorcade as it approached Army House in Rawalpindi. When the van was blown to smithereens, just as the president's car passed, it destroyed several nearby vehicles and damaged other armored cars in the motorcade. The atmosphere was black with smoke. The scene was one of bloody carnage, of glass and metal shards flying through the air.

Seconds later, another van being driven by a suicide bomber lurched from the side of the road. A police van rammed it before it could crash into Musharraf's car. Both vans were blown to pieces, and the president's driver instinctively slammed on

This is the scene of a December 2003 car bomb attack from which Musharraf narrowly escaped death. Fourteen people, including six police officers, were killed.

the brakes. "Dabaa! Dabaa!" The car's tires had blown out, but at Musharraf's repeated yell, the driver forced it forward on the rims. They reached the safety of Army House.

Fourteen people died in the attack, including six police officers. Investigators soon linked the assassination plot to Al Qaeda terrorists operating inside Pakistan.

The date—December 25, 2003, the day Westerners were celebrating as Christmas—may not have been coincidental. Radical Muslims consider Musharraf a traitor to Islam. To them, he has befriended the Christian West and helped the United States exert control in Islamic territories—notably in Pakistan, Afghanistan, and Iraq. Musharraf's removal, they believe, is necessary to liberate the region from the military and economic influences of Western powers.

A similar attack had occurred just eleven days earlier. On December 14—the day American forces captured Saddam Hussein in Iraq—a bomb exploded a bridge a split second after Musharraf's car crossed it. Musharraf was arriving home from a trip and was only 500 yards (457 meters) from Army House. The car was hurled into the air, but because of its protective armor, none of the passengers were injured.

After the bombings that almost claimed his life, travel security for Musharraf naturally was

stepped up. When he travels by car, his routes
and destinations are kept top secret and all
other traffic is blocked from the routes his
motorcade takes. Still, new plots are devised,
using different weapons. Musharraf understands
that he is never truly safe. He repeatedly has
expressed his conviction that Allah has protected
and supported him. As evidence, he cites not
only his harrowing escapes from accidents and
assassination plots, but his ability to cast out the
Sharif government.

INTERNAL DIFFICULTIES

Pakistan is an Islamic country. What sets it
apart from other nations dominated by Muslim
populations is that it was created to be an
Islamic republic. Musharraf is a Muslim but is
considered a modernist who does not follow
strict interpretations of Islamic law. Both he
and his wife, Sebha, are regarded as moderate,
even liberal, in their Islamic faith, compared to
fundamentalists. For example, he occasionally
drinks alcoholic beverages, which are forbidden
in Islamic countries. He has challenged the

devout clerics of Islam to ease the severity of their teachings and to eliminate materials that endorse hatred of others. He has pushed for a government that is tolerant to all ethnic groups and religions. Because of these views, he is unpopular among Muslim fundamentalists.

They are even more incensed that he took the side of the United States in confronting Afghanistan's Taliban regime. With the over-throw of their government, many former Taliban soldiers in Afghanistan slipped across the border and joined Islamic extremist bands in Pakistan. They consider Musharraf a one-time supporter who turned against them.

Anti-Western terrorist groups in Pakistan began carrying out attacks within weeks after the September 2001 U.S.-Pakistani alliance. Forty people were killed when armed men raided the state assembly building in Srinagar in Jammu and Kashmir in October. Two months later, commandos assaulted the Indian Parliament building in New Delhi, killing six people. Although the attackers' identities were undetermined, Indians believed they were backed by Pakistani authorities. Musharraf strongly denied the charge. To demonstrate his opposition to such acts, he ordered the arrests of some 2,000 Muslim militants and banned two of the main radical Muslim organizations that were operating in Pakistan.

Terrorism continues. Car bombings and raids have ravaged such targets as the U.S. consulate in Karachi and Christian gatherings. Non-Muslims, mainly Hindus and Christians, make up a slight minority of Pakistan's population— about 3 percent. Officially, they are entitled to worship as they wish. In practice, numerous reports of Muslims persecuting non-Muslims have come out of Pakistan. In one attack, eighteen people were shot while attending a church service in Punjab in 2001. Musharraf has attempted to control militant groups believed to be responsible for religious repression and violence, but the threats remain.

The presence of Muslim extremists inside Pakistan has cast it as a nation of terrorists, in the eyes of many outsiders, Musharraf complains. He contends that the problem began in 1979, when the United States and other Western countries helped Pakistan organize and arm thousands of mujahideen guerrilla fighters to confront the Soviets who had invaded Afghanistan. When the Soviets withdrew a decade later, Afghanistan was left under the control of the Taliban, with some 30,000 equipped and combat-experienced Muslim militants.

COPING WITH TERRORISM

Musharraf says Pakistan opposes terrorism not because it necessarily agrees with U.S. policies but to protect its own interests. He has had thousands of Al Qaeda leaders and soldiers in Pakistan arrested during the last five years. He has stated, however, that it will take long-term social and economic improvements, not just military action, to abolish terrorism. Many of the disbanded terrorist organizations have re-established themselves, sometimes under new names. They mingle with civilians, making it difficult for authorities to deal with them. For instance, in October 2006, the government ordered an air strike against an Islamic boarding school near the Afghanistan border; the school apparently was being used as a base of operations by a Taliban rebel group. School children reportedly were among the eighty people killed in the attack. Terrorists responded with bombing attacks that killed some fifty soldiers, civilians, and a tribal leader who had been working with the government to quash militant activities.

To Musharraf, Al Qaeda members who operate from within Pakistan are violating his country's sovereignty. But even as Musharraf has joined the international fight against violent radicals, journalists have reported evidence that his own intelligence agency secretly has assisted remnants of the Taliban. Equally disturbing is that some of the officers and soldiers in Pakistan's army oppose Musharraf's policies. They do not like carrying out his orders to arrest Muslim fundamentalist leaders and break up terrorist training camps. A great international fear is that Muslim extremists are growing in number within Pakistan's military. Some believe it is only a matter of time before the radicals control the country's army—and its nuclear weapons. They also fear

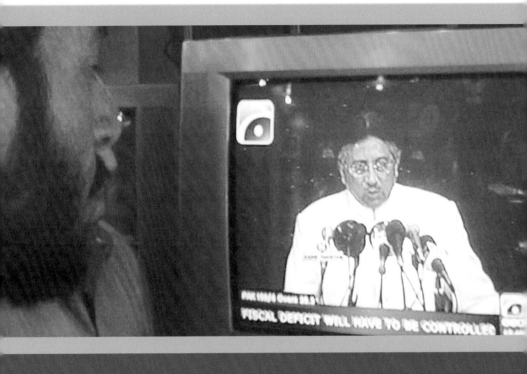

Musharraf makes a televised speech to the Pakistan
National Assembly in January 2004. He recently had won
a vote of confidence from the country's electoral college.

that because of its weak economy, Pakistan may
be tempted to sell nuclear secrets and materials
to nations ruled by extremists.

EXERTING FIRM CONTROL

Although Islamic fundamentalists regard him
as too soft, Musharraf has also come under

criticism from within and outside Pakistan for using a heavy hand. He has been accused of forcing out members of the supreme court who challenged the legality of his coup. Many observers believe the referendum of April 2002 was manipulated in his favor. And critics question the validity of some of his constitutional amendments. For example, Musharraf has obtained the authority to dismiss the National Assembly and the prime minister.

A major point of contention has been Musharraf's insistence on remaining commander in chief of the army while serving as president. In 2004, he agreed to turn over the military post to a successor. By the end of the year, however, he had gotten a law passed by the National Assembly allowing him to continue as both head of state and head of the military. To justify his decision, he points to the combination of issues confronting the government. Some examples include the war against terror, relations with India, internal problems with tribes and political factions, and criticism of the country's nuclear program. "With all this facing Pakistan, with so many pulls in different directions, there was a dire need for unity of command in governance," he explains in his book, *In the Line of Fire.*

In January 2004, Musharraf called for a vote of confidence by Pakistan's electoral college. He won more than half the ballots. Although legal experts questioned whether the vote was valid, it entitles him to hold the office of president until October 2007.

Many observers wonder whether Musharraf will, in fact, step down when the current term ends. Others, reflecting on the spate of assassination attempts, grimly wonder whether he will survive that long.

CHAPTER EIGHT

"IN THE LINE OF FIRE"

Musharraf flew to the United States in September 2006—and into a firestorm of questions and controversy. His book, *In the Line of Fire: A Memoir*, was about to be released. Political commentators were especially eager to interpret his statements concerning Pakistan's attitude toward India and its role in the U.S.-led war on terrorism.

Musharraf spoke at the United Nations in New York City, met with President George W. Bush, then flew to London and met with Prime Minister Tony Blair of Great Britain. The purpose of his trip was to discuss such international issues as trade, intelligence concerns, and counterterrorism. Much of the media coverage, however, was devoted to his memoir—a remarkable publication because memoirs typically are written by heads of state after they leave office.

In the Line of Fire, Musharraf's memoir, was published in the United States in September 2006 and became an immediate best seller.

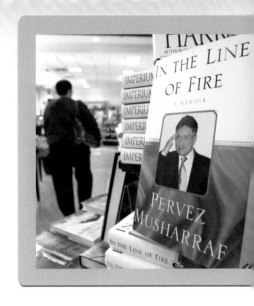

   In his book, Musharraf says that on the morning after the September 2001 terrorist attacks against United States targets, he received an urgent phone call from U.S. secretary of state Colin Powell. "You are either with us or against us," Powell reputedly told him. Meanwhile, Musharraf writes, after talking with a member of Powell's staff, U.S. deputy secretary of state Richard Armitage, the Pakistani intelligence director said that "we had to decide whether we were with America or with the terrorists, but that if we chose the terrorists, then we should be prepared to be bombed back to the

Stone Age." The latter statement made head-lines, although it was common knowledge that Musharraf had been under intense pressure to side with the United States in the antiterror campaign.

Although Musharraf's alliance with the United States has increased his peril, in certain ways it has produced positive effects for him and for Pakistan. Internationally, Musharraf no longer is perceived as a military dictator who ousted an elected prime minister, but as a popular head of state who is willing to risk his life for a just cause. His nation's economy has benefited not only from the lifting of economic sanctions but from approximately $3 billion in foreign aid—a substantial reward for its cooperation.

PAKISTAN'S INTERNAL PROBLEMS

Apart from the tremendous dangers of the war on terrorism, Musharraf faces numerous problems as Pakistan's leader. It is a nation of many ethnic groups with different, often conflicting, interests. They speak more than 300 languages. Even before the area that now is Pakistan became an independent country, it was a scene of tension and violence.

Pakistan's people vary from rich property holders to merchants and business owners, rural herders, and peasants. Many people languish in poverty. Their diversity complicates the task of maintaining law and order. In some provinces, people are ruled more by age-old systems of tribal leadership than by the national government. Many do not think of themselves as Pakistanis, but as Punjabis, Sindhis, Pashtuns, Baluchis, etc. Some ethnic groups have been rivals for many generations.

Musharraf's government also must cope with problems of nature. An example is high levels of salt content in agricultural land and irrigation water. This results largely from the country's large-scale irrigation systems, which use diverted river water rather than rainfall. Too much salt content can cause fields to become infertile.

Deforestation—the loss of natural forests— is a growing concern. Less than 5 percent of the country is in forests. Many Pakistanis depend on wood for heating. Coupled with commercial timber cutting, this is causing Pakistan's woodlands to dwindle.

Pollution caused by factories and automobiles is another environmental problem. Gradually, the country has been adapting automobiles to CNG (compressed natural gas). Happily for Pakistanis, natural gas—less polluting than oil-based fuels—is one of the country's significant resources.

The economy has been problematic throughout Pakistan's history. A substantial portion of Pakistan's national income is provided by Pakistanis who live and work in foreign countries, sending money to relatives back home.

THE WORLD'S VIEW OF PAKISTAN

International headaches besides terrorism also confront Musharraf. Pakistan's nuclear weapons program has resulted in sanctions and international disdain. Pakistan has been working on nuclear projects since the 1960s. In May 1998, both India and Pakistan conducted atomic bomb tests, which were denounced by the United States and other countries.

Musharraf contends that Pakistan's nuclear program was started in response to that of India. "Now, ever since Pakistan followed India into the nuclear club, the world holds its breath at our every confrontation," he writes in his memoir. "This situation is much worse than the Cold War, which was fought at a distance. . . . When your enemy is your neighbor, when you have fought open wars repeatedly, when you are in dispute over a large piece of territory, and when your historical memory is rooted in mutual slaughter from the founding of your nation, you face not a cold war, but a deadly embrace, with guns drawn and fingers on the triggers."

The global community is worried not only about the specter of a nuclear war between Pakistan and India, but about the security of Pakistan's nuclear secrets. In 2003, a chilling scandal engulfed the country when it was revealed that a Pakistani scientist, Dr. A. Q. Khan, had sold nuclear technology and plans to Iran, North Korea, and Libya during the 1980s and 1990s. Khan had become a national hero for his leadership in Pakistan's nuclear development

Dr. A. Q. Khan, mastermind of Pakistan's nuclear arms program, made news when it was revealed he had leaked nuclear secrets to other countries. Musharraf pardoned the scientist.

program. After an internal investigation confirmed the allegations, Musharraf pardoned him and placed him in protective custody.

Musharraf rightfully can claim significant achievements as Pakistan's leader. Despite the unceasing tension between Pakistan and India, Musharraf stated in early 2006 that relations between them are better than they've ever been since independence. Observers have noted encouraging signals toward an ease in tension during the past few years. They include the formal cease-fire agreed on in 2003; diplomatic dialogue; and the resuming of bus transportation across the border. A July 2006 bombing in the Indian port of Mumbai (formerly called Bombay) killed almost 200 people and temporarily suspended peace talks. In September, however, Musharraf and Indian prime minister Manmohan Singh met and agreed to renew negotiations. They also planned to create an Indo-Pakistani antiterror agency.

In December 2006, Musharraf stepped up his efforts to resolve the border conflict. He proposed that both Pakistan and India withdraw all forces from the disputed region and leave the people there to govern their own affairs, in large part. However, his plan called for both countries to retain a degree of supervision in the disputed area rather than grant the region complete independence.

Meanwhile, Musharraf has opened diplomatic communications with Israel (a move resented by radical Muslims). He explains that although he,

Musharraf and Prime Minister Manmohan Singh of India announce renewed negotiations between their countries after a September 2006 meeting in Cuba.

like other Islamic leaders, favors the formation of a separate Palestine, he also recognizes Israel as a sovereign state.

A DANGEROUS ROLE

Musharraf's position as Pakistan's head of state clearly is one of the most difficult and dangerous jobs in the world. The title he chose for his memoirs is appropriate; perhaps to a greater extent than any other world leader, Pervez Musharraf lives "in the line of fire." Threats come not only from terrorists but from inside the ranks of his own army. As recently as October 2006, rockets exploded near his residence in Rawalpindi. Junior officers in the Pakistan military were arrested as suspects.

In the face of insecurities and threats from without and within, Musharraf is hopeful for his country. He believes progress has been made toward peace and prosperity, though much remains to be done. He concludes in his memoir: "With determination, persistence, and honest patriotic zeal, God willing, we will become a dynamic, progressive, and moderate Islamic state, and a useful member of the international comity of nations—a state that is a model to be emulated, not shunned."

TIMELINE

1943 August 11, Pervez Musharraf is born in New Delhi.

1947 Musharraf's family flees to Karachi in the new nation of Pakistan; the First Indo-Pakistani War is waged.

1949 The family relocates to Turkey, where Musharraf's father is assigned to the Pakistani embassy in Ankara.

1956 The family returns to Karachi.

1958 General Muhammad Ayub Khan takes over the presidency of Pakistan, beginning a long period of military rule.

1961 Musharraf serves valiantly in the Second Indo-Pakistani War.

1968 Musharraf marries Sehba Farid.

1971 East Pakistan fights for its independence and becomes Bangladesh.

1977 General Muhammad Zia ul-Haq seizes control of the government of Pakistan.

1988 Zia is killed in a plane crash; Benazir Bhutto is elected prime minister.

1990 Musharraf is sent to the Royal College of Defence Studies in London, England.

1991 After Benazir Bhutto is deposed, Nawaz Sharif becomes Pakistan's prime minister.

1993 Sharif resigns; Bhutto again becomes prime minister.

1995 Musharraf is promoted to lieutenant general.

1997 Sharif again becomes prime minister after Bhutto is ousted from office.

1998 Sharif appoints Musharraf chief of the army; Pakistan and India test nuclear weapons, heightening international anxiety.

1999 The army deposes Prime Minister Sharif; Musharraf becomes leader of the country.

2001 Musharraf declares himself president; later in the year, he joins the United States in the war against terrorism.

2002 A national referendum approves a five-year extension of Musharraf's presidency; elections are held for the National Assembly and provincial government representatives and for prime minister.

2003 The Pakistan National Assembly meets for the first time since Musharraf's takeover; Musharraf survives two assassination attempts.

2004 Musharraf wins an electoral college vote to remain in office until 2007.

2006 Musharraf renews negotiations with India; he meets with leaders in the United States and Great Britain; his book, *In the Line of Fire: A Memoir*, is published; he survives a rocket attack by assassins.

Glossary

academics Educational studies.

artillery Heavy weapons including rocket launchers, cannons, and mortars.

atrocity A barbarous act.

cleric A religious leader.

Cold War The state of tension between democratic and Communist superpowers that existed during the late twentieth century.

colonialism The occupation and control by one country of a distant territory.

comity of nations Mutual respect and courtesy among nations and governments.

commando A soldier who is specially trained to make secret raids behind enemy lines.

coup d'état The takeover of a government or leadership position by force.

court-martial A trial by a military court.

customs service The government agency that oversees imported items.

despot An oppressive leader.

effigy A picture, sculpture, or other form of mock likeness of a person.

embassy The building or compound, often located in a nation's capital, where the diplomats and staff of a foreign nation work.

faction A small group that seeks control over or within a larger group.

foreign office A government department that handles international relations.

guerrilla A soldier in an independent force that is not attached to a government, seeking to inflict damage often by sabotage or other terrorist tactics.

jihad A holy war declared by Muslims against non-Muslims; the word "jihad" may be translated literally as "striving."

martial law Law enforced by the military, typically in times of crisis.

mujahideen Muslims who fight a jihad (holy war); also called "freedom fighters."

sanctions Measures taken by one nation (or nations) to exert pressure on another nation that is thought to be acting outside the common good.

Shia Muslims who believe that only the descendants of Ali, son-in-law of the prophet Muhammad, are the rightful leaders of Islam.

Sikh An independent Hindu sect.

sovereignty A nation's right and power to rule itself, uninfluenced by outsiders.

stalemate The end of a conflict in which neither side has won a significant advantage.

Sunni The Muslim majority who believe the leaders of Islam should be chosen by consensus, not by ancestral links to Ali, who was the son-in-law of the prophet Muhammad.

For More Information

The Asia Foundation
465 California Street, 9th Floor
San Francisco, CA 94104
(415) 982-4640
Web site: http://www.asiafoundation.org

Hidaya Foundation
1766 Scott Boulevard, Suite 115
Santa Clara, CA 95050
(408) 244-3282
(866) 2HIDAYA (244-3292)
Web site: http://www.hidaya.org

Human Development Foundation
1350 Remington Road, Suite W
Schaumburg, IL 60173
(800) 705-1310
Web site: http://www.yespakistan.com/hdf

National Fund for Cultural Heritage
Ministry of Culture, 11th Floor
Green Tower, Blue Area, F-6/3
Islamabad
Pakistan
Web site: http://www.heritage.gov.pk

Pakistan Literacy Fund
45 West 60th Street, Suite 22K
New York, NY 10023
(917) 373-3473
Web site: http://www.pakfund.org

President of Pakistan
Web site: http://www.presidentofpakistan.gov.pk

WEB SITES

Due to the changing nature of Internet links,
Rosen Publishing has developed an online list of
Web sites related to the subject of this book.
This site is updated regularly. Please use this link
to access the list:

http://www.rosenlinks.com/nm/pemu

For Further Reading

Black, Carolyn. *Pakistan—the People* (Lands, People, and Cultures). New York, NY: Crabtree Publishing Company, 2002.

Crompton, Samuel Willard. *Pakistan* (Modern World Nations). Broomall, PA: Chelsea House, 2002.

Greenberger, Robert. *A Historical Atlas of Pakistan*. New York, NY: The Rosen Publishing Group, Inc., 2003.

Haque, Jameel. *Pakistan* (Countries of the World). Milwaukee, WI: Gareth Stevens Publishing, 2002.

Kras, Sara Louise. *Pervez Musharraf* (Major World Leaders). Philadelphia, PA: Chelsea House Publishers, 2004.

Malik, Iftikhar H. *Culture and Customs of Pakistan* (Culture and Customs of Asia). Westport, CT: Greenwood Press, 2005.

Rorabak, Amanda. *Pakistan in a Nutshell* (The World in a Nutshell). Santa Monica, CA: Enisen Publishing, 2004.

Sheehan, Sean, and Shahrezad Samiuddin. *Pakistan* (Cultures of the World). 2nd ed. New York, NY: Marshall Cavendish, 2004.

Taus-Bolstad, Stacy. *Pakistan in Pictures* (Visual Geography). Minneapolis, MN: Lerner Publishing Group, 2003.

Wagner, Heather Lehr. *India and Pakistan* (People at Odds). Broomall, PA: Chelsea House, 2002.

Bibliography

Bergen, Peter L. *Holy War, Inc.: Inside the Secret World of Osama bin Laden*. New York, NY: The Free Press, 2001.

Blood, Peter R., ed. *Pakistan: A Country Study*. 6th ed. Washington, DC: Federal Research Division, Library of Congress, 1995.

Bodansky, Yossef. *Bin Laden: The Man Who Declared War on America*. Rocklin, CA: Forum, 1999.

Giacomo, Carol. *"Musharraf Upbeat on Talks with India."* Reuters. Retrieved September 2006 (http://www.boston.com/news/world/asia/ articles/2006/09/19/musharraf_upbeat_on_talks _with_india/?rss_id=Boston.com+%2F+News).

Kras, Sara Louise. *Pervez Musharraf* (Major World Leaders). Philadelphia, PA: Chelsea House Publishers, 2004.

Musharraf, Pervez. *In the Line of Fire: A Memoir*. New York, NY: Free Press, 2006.

"Pakistan." The World Factbook. Retrieved
November 20, 2006 (https://www.cia.gov/
cia/publications/factbook/geos/pk.html).

"President Pervez Musharraf." BBC News.
Retrieved September 2006 (http://newsvote.
bbc.co.uk/mpapps/pagetools/print/news.bbc.co.
uk/1/hi/world/south_asia/1742997.stm).

"Q&A: Pervez Musharraf, President of Pakistan."
Washingtonpost.com. Retrieved October 2006
(http://www.washingtonpost.com/wp-dyn/
content/article/2006/01/27/AR2006012701350
_pf.html).

Wolpert, Stanley. Roots of Confrontation in South
Asia: Afghanistan, Pakistan, India and the
Superpowers. New York, NY: Oxford
University Press, 1982.

Index

ABOUT THE AUTHOR

Daniel E. Harmon has written numerous books, primarily histories, international and social studies, and biographies. Recent works include country studies of Kyrgyzstan, Turkey, and Libya, and a biography of Ayatollah Ruhollah Khomeini. He previously wrote six volumes about the colonial period in Africa. Harmon is a veteran magazine and newspaper editor and writer whose articles have appeared in many national and regional periodicals.

PHOTO CREDITS

Cover, pp. 20, 23, 25, 28, 37, 39, 59, 74 © Getty Images; pp. 4–5, 33, 43, 51, 63, 66, 69, 78, 85, 89, 94, 96 © AFP/Getty Images; p. 12 © Time Life Pictures/Getty Images; p. 15 Tahara Anderson for The Rosen Publishing Group; p. 17 © Bettmann/Corbis; p. 45 © Galen Rowell/ Corbis; p. 54 © Reuters/Corbis.

Designer: Gene Mollica; **Editor:** Kathy Kuhtz Campbell
Photo Researcher: Cindy Reiman